W9-AUY-634

ω 3/22

OC - - '14

DISCARD

# A Benjamin Blog
## and His Inquisitive Dog
# Guide

PROPERTY OF C.L.P.L

# China

Anita Ganeri

Heinemann
LIBRARY

Chicago, Illinois

© 2015 Heinemann Library
an imprint of Capstone Global Library, LLC
Chicago, Illinois

All rights reserved. No part of this publication may
be reproduced or transmitted in any form or by
any means, electronic or mechanical, including
photocopying, recording, taping, or any information
storage and retrieval system, without permission in
writing from the publisher.

Edited by Dan Nunn, Helen Cox Cannons,
and Gina Kammer
Designed by Jo Hinton-Malivoire
Picture research by Ruth Blair and Hannah Taylor
Production by Helen McCreath
Originated by Capstone Global Library Ltd
Printed and bound in Dubai by Oriental Press

18 17 16 15 14
10 9 8 7 6 5 4 3 2 1

Library of Congress
Cataloging-in-Publication Data
Cataloging-in-publication information is on file with
the Library of Congress.
ISBN 978-1-4109-6661-2 (hardcover)
ISBN 978-1-4109-6670-4 (paperback)
ISBN 978-1-4109-6688-9 (eBook PDF)

Acknowledgments
We would like to thank the following for permission to
reproduce photographs:

Alamy: dierming, 16, icpix_hk, 18, Image Source, 14,
LatitudeStock, 6, Mooch Images, 19, Ron Yue, 27;
Getty Images: AFP, 25, China Tourism Press, 8, Jade, 20;
Shutterstock: 06photo, 12, Alan Bailey, 21, BassKwong,
13, Eastimages, 7, Hung Chung Chih, cover, 22, 24,
leungchopan, 17, Monkey Business Images, 15, Pal
Teravagimov, 9, Paul Stringer, 28, ProfStocker, 10,
silver-john, 11, Songquan Deng, 26, 29, testing, 23;
Superstock: Pixtal, 4

Every effort has been made to contact copyright
holders of material reproduced in this book. Any
omissions will be rectified in subsequent printings if
notice is given to the publisher.

All the Internet addresses (URLs) given in this book
were valid at the time of going to press. However, due
to the dynamic nature of the Internet, some addresses
may have changed, or sites may have changed or
ceased to exist since publication. While the author
and publisher regret any inconvenience this may
cause readers, no responsibility for any such changes
can be accepted by either the author or the publisher.

007015ORISF14

Some words are shown in bold, **like this.** You can find
out what they mean by looking in the glossary.

# Contents

# Welcome to China!

Hello! My name is Benjamin Blog and this is Barko Polo, my **inquisitive** dog. (He is named after ancient ace explorer, **Marco Polo**.) We have just gotten back from our latest adventure—exploring China. We put this book together from some of the blog posts we wrote on the way.

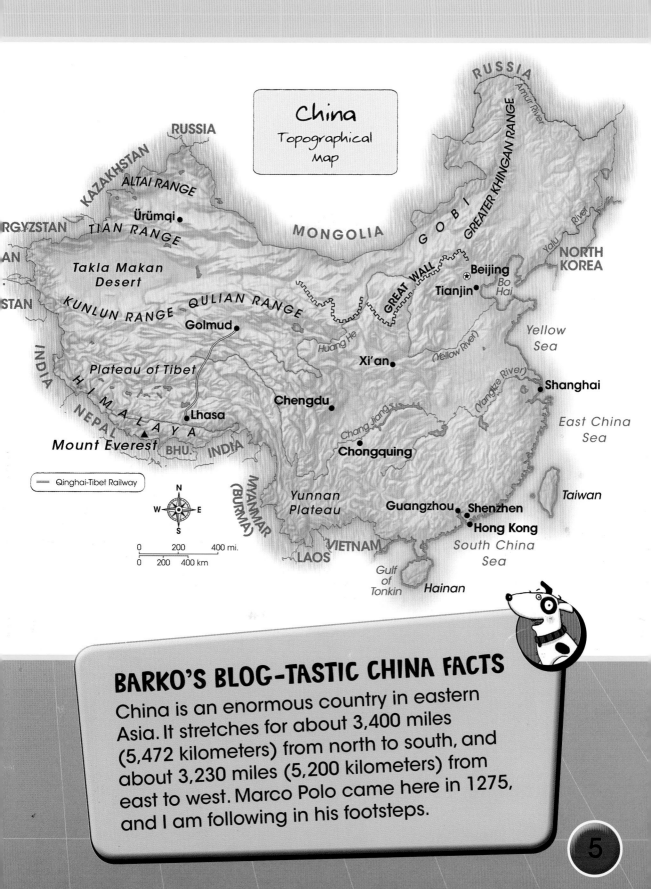

## China
### Topographical Map

RUSSIA

KAZAKHSTAN

ALTAI RANGE

Ürümqi

RGYZSTAN

TIAN RANGE

AN

Takla Makan
Desert

STAN

KUNLUN RANGE

QULIAN RANGE

Golmud

INDIA

Plateau of Tibet

NEPAL

HIMALAYA

Lhasa

Mount Everest

BHU.

INDIA

MYANMAR
(BURMA)

Yunnan
Plateau

LAOS

VIETNAM

Gulf
of
Tonkin

Hainan

MONGOLIA

GOBI

GREATER KHINGAN RANGE

RUSSIA

Amur River

GREAT WALL

Yalu River

NORTH
KOREA

Beijing

Tianjin

Bo
Hai

Huang He

Xi'an

(Yellow River)

Yellow
Sea

Chengdu

Chang Jiang

(Yangtze River)

Shanghai

East China
Sea

Chongquing

Guangzhou

Shenzhen

Hong Kong

Taiwan

South China
Sea

Qinghai-Tibet Railway

N
W E
S

0    200    400 mi.
0    200    400 km

# BARKO'S BLOG-TASTIC CHINA FACTS

China is an enormous country in eastern
Asia. It stretches for about 3,400 miles
(5,472 kilometers) from north to south, and
about 3,230 miles (5,200 kilometers) from
east to west. Marco Polo came here in 1275,
and I am following in his footsteps.

# Armies and Games

Posted by: Ben Blog | September 1 at 10:32 a.m.

The first stop on our tour was the city of Xi'an and one of the most famous sights in China—the terra-cotta army. More than 2,000 years ago, Qin Shi Huangdi became **emperor** of China. When he died, he was buried in a **tomb** guarded by thousands of life-sized clay soldiers.

## BARKO'S BLOG-TASTIC CHINA FACTS

In 2008, the Olympic Games were held in Beijing. This is the amazing **stadium** where many of the events were held. It is known as the Bird's Nest Stadium. Can you guess why?

# Deserts, Mountains, and Rivers

Posted by: Ben Blog | September 12 at 6:13 a.m.

From Xi'an, we headed northwest to the Takla Makan Desert. This huge desert is covered in **sand dunes** that are always moving, burying homes and villages. It is baking hot by day, freezing cold at night, and dry as a bone. Not a place to get myself lost in!

## BARKO'S BLOG-TASTIC CHINA FACTS

Mount Everest, the highest mountain on Earth, stands between the Tibetan region of China and Nepal. It is 29,035 feet (8,850 meters) tall, so there is no way that I am climbing to the top.

After the heat and dust of the desert, it was good to be near water again. Barko took this photo of me by the Yangtze, the longest river in China and in all of Asia. It flows for about 3,915 miles (6,300 kilometers) and is called *Chang Jiang* in Chinese, which means "Long River."

## BARKO'S BLOG-TASTIC CHINA FACTS

Giant pandas live in **bamboo** forests on a few mountains in southwest China. They have to eat for up to 16 hours a day to get enough bamboo shoots and leaves to fill them up.

# City Tour

Posted by: Ben Blog | October 24 at 11:35 p.m.

Our next stop was Beijing, the capital city of China. About half of all Chinese people live in cities, and about 20 million live in Beijing. I am off to visit the Forbidden City, which was once the **emperor's** palace. I have been told that the best way to get there is by bike.

# BARKO'S BLOG-TASTIC CHINA FACTS

With 23 million people, Shanghai is China's biggest city. It is located on the east coast of China at the **mouth** of the Yangtze River and is one of the world's most important **ports**.

13

# Ni Hao!

Posted by: Ben Blog | November 10 at 7:37 a.m.

More than 1.3 billion people live in China—more than in any other country. Most people speak Mandarin Chinese. *Ni hao* means "hello." Chinese is written in symbols, called characters. Each character stands for a different word or idea.

## BARKO'S BLOG-TASTIC CHINA FACTS

Families are quite small in China and most people only have one child. Children are expected to show **respect** to other people, especially to older people, such as grandparents.

These Chinese children are doing their exercises before school begins. In China, children start school at about the age of 6, and they are expected to work hard. They study subjects such as Chinese, math, science, history, music, and physical education.

## BARKO'S BLOG-TASTIC CHINA FACTS

In Chinese cities, most people live in huge blocks of apartments. Their apartments are small with no yards, but most cities have parks where people can walk, bicycle, fly kites, and keep fit.

We have arrived in Hong Kong in time for Chinese New Year! It is the most important holiday in China, and the dancing is wonderful. The dancers are dressed as a dragon, and they twist and turn their way through the streets. In China, dragons are thought to bring good luck.

## BARKO'S BLOG-TASTIC CHINA FACTS

China does not have an official religion, but many people follow Buddhism, Taoism, and Confucianism, which are each thousands of years old. This is a Taoist temple in Chengdu.

# Feeling Hungry

Posted by: Ben Blog | February 4 at 12:31 p.m.

China is so enormous that each part of the country has its own special foods. We have come to Guangdong in the southeast to try out dim sum. Dim sum are bite-sized snacks, such as dumplings, buns filled with meat, and stuffed lotus leaves. Tasty!

## BARKO'S BLOG-TASTIC CHINA FACTS

Chinese people use **chopsticks** to eat their meals. You must hold them the right way, though, or it is bad manners.

# Opera and Kung Fu

Posted by: Ben Blog | February 19 at 7:29 p.m.

Today, we went back to Beijing and made a trip to the opera. Chinese opera is very popular and dates back more than 1,000 years. Characters wear masks and spectacular costumes. The show is a mixture of music, singing, **mime**, dancing, and acrobatics.

**BARKO'S BLOG-TASTIC CHINA FACTS**

Kung fu is a famous Chinese **martial art**. It is a set of movements and exercises that are meant to improve a person's body and mind. I wonder if it works on dogs?

23

# From Paddy Fields to Toy Factories

Posted by: Ben Blog | February 22 at 4:56 p.m.

Nearly half of Chinese people work in farming, and rice is one of the most important crops. More rice is grown in China than in any other country. Here, in Hubei, you can see the rice growing in flooded **paddy fields**. Most of it is still picked by hand, which is very hard work.

## BARKO'S BLOG-TASTIC CHINA FACTS

If you look at a toy in a toy store, it has probably been made in China. China has thousands of factories making toys, DVD players, mobile phones, shoes, clothes, and much more.

# And Finally ...

Posted by: Ben Blog | March 7 at 8:18 a.m.

It is the last day of our tour, and we are at the Great Wall of China. It stretches for more than 5,500 miles (8,850 kilometers), and some of it dates back more than 2,000 years. Some parts are crumbling, but I am off to find a part that I can walk along. Coming with me, Barko?

## BARKO'S BLOG-TASTIC CHINA FACTS

We also went on a boat trip up the Yangtze River to see the huge Three Gorges **Dam**. It was opened in 2012, and it is the biggest dam in the world. It uses river water to make electricity.

# China Fact File

Area: 3,694,959 square miles
(9,569,901 square kilometers)

Population: 1,349,585,838 (2013)

Capital city: Beijing

Other main cities: Shanghai; Chongqing;
Shenzhen

Language: Mandarin Chinese

Main religions: Buddhism; Taoism; Confucianism

Highest mountain: Mount Everest
(29,035 feet/8,850 meters)

Longest river: Yangtze
(3,915 miles/6,300 kilometers)

Currency: Renminbi (yuan)

# China Quiz

Find out how much you know about China with our quick quiz.

1. Which is the biggest city in China?
a) Beijing
b) Shanghai
c) Wuhan

2. What do giant pandas eat?
a) rice
b) meat
c) bamboo

3. What does *ni hao* mean?
a) good-bye
b) hello
c) how are you?

4. What are dim sum?
a) Chinese snacks
b) Chinese boats
c) Chinese hats

5. What is this?

5. Great Wall of China
4. a
3. b
2. c
1. b
**Answers**

# Glossary

**bamboo** a tall plant with a thin, woody stem

**chopstick** a wooden stick used to eat food

**dam** a high wall built across a river to stop it flowing

**emperor** a ruler of China in ancient times

**inquisitive** being interested in learning about the world

**Marco Polo** an explorer who lived from about 1254 to 1324; he traveled from Italy to China

**martial art** a kind of sport, such as judo or karate

**mime** a way of acting things out without using words

**mouth** a place where a river flows into the sea

**paddy field** a flooded field where rice is grown

**port** a town or city next to a river or the sea, where ships load and unload goods

**respect** being polite and helpful to someone else

**sand dune** a giant heap of sand, piled up by the wind

**stadium** a place where sports are played, with seats for spectators

**tomb** a place where a dead person's body is placed

# Find Out More

## Books

James, Oliver. *China* (Countries in Our World).
Mankato: Smart Apple Media, 2011

Mattern, Joanne. *We Visit China*
(Your Land and My Land).
Hockessin,Del.: Mitchell Lane Publishers, 2014

Savery, Annabel. *China* (Been There!).
Mankato: Smart Apple Media, 2012

## Websites

**kids.nationalgeographic.com/kids/places**
The National Geographic website has lots of
information, photos, and maps of countries around
the world.

**www.worldatlas.com**
Packed with information about various countries,
this website includes flags, time zones, facts, maps,
and timelines.

# Index